"CHUCKLING POETRY" plus

BY

GARNET DURHAM

G
GWD
D

*for IAN
Happy Reading*

Published by

Durham & Durham Books
60 Highbury, Newcastle upon Tyne
NE2 3IN

and

Bergh Apton
Bramber, Steyning, West Sussex
BN44 3PQ

First Edition

ISBN 0-9549431-0-4

Printed in Great Britain by Gemini Press
Unit 1 Dolphin Road Industrial Site
Shoreham-by-Sea
West Sussex BN43 6NZ

AUTHOR'S EXCUSE

I have been composing poetry for many years to amuse my family, our grandchildren and friends. When Mike Tarry, our eldest grandson commented he had received enough poetry to fill a book, the idea to publish was born. I distributed pamphlets with a random selection of poems to folk I met during the next month. The answers were encouraging. Some of the comments are recorded below:

"Well done, I like this sort of poetry. Shakespeare you are not, but I had enough of him at school!" *Ron Adams, Crowborough!*

"Enormous fun reading your poems. Can we nominate you for Poet Laureate!" *Ross and Rosemary Windebank, Steyning*

"I particularly like the poem about the robin - I read it aloud at a coffee morning, they insisted I read it again." *Mary Townsend, Steyning*

"We enjoyed reading your poems. How do you do it? – You should publish a book." *David Arnold, Shoreham-by-Sea*

"May I congratulate on your poems, present Poet Laureate beware! We enjoyed the wide variety and wish you every encouragement" *Yvonne Campbell, London*

"Thank you for your charming poem, it certainly did bring a smile to my face (made me chuckle actually!)" *TV weather girl!*

"Good stuff!" *BBC news presenter*

"Your poems certainly brightened up my day"! *Diane Taylor, Steyning*

"I much enjoyed your poetry, especially Appointments" *Michael Lee, London*

"The Blood Ladies is super. I pinned it up on the wall over my desk. I read it every morning and smile before I begin taking blood samples" *Breda Dewar, Ireland*

"Humourous and entertaining!" *Valerie Haben, Doctor's secretary*

"These are really, really good, I like them very much. The one about Appointments is super!" *Dental receptionist*

"Our boys had a hilarious bedtime noisily finishing your Ode to a Baked Bean (Unfinished)." *Jennifer Clayton, Worthing*

"Excellent, I really enjoyed them. More please! *Dentist, Shoreham by Sea*

"There are several that would go down very well at the rugby club" *Mike Goulding*

"Received and enjoyed" *Frank Smith*

CONTENTS

A POEM ABOUT A ROBIN

I've just made friends with a robin,
It was ever so easy to do.
I started to dig in my garden
When down beside me he flew.

I am just making friends with a robin,
His breast is as red as can be
He flits to and fro, as I dig every row
He gets closer and closer to me.

I hope I have made friends with a robin,
Who seems hungry as hungry can be
His appetite for worms is enormous
Is it worms he loves and not me?

I'm sure I've made friends with this robin,
He seems ever so friendly to me
Here's hoping he comes back tomorrow
I will just have to be patient and see.

I have really made friends with this robin –
He has come back with all of his friends
Plus four and twenty blackbirds
So here the nice verse ends.

Watching this robin flit about
He must find the worms delicious
My robin looks so healthy
The worms must be nutritious

If you would like to make friends with a robin
I am sure he would make friends with you
You are welcome to help dig my garden
There is still such a lot to do.

SITTING IN THE GARDEN

I have mown the lawn, trimmed the edges,
Repaired the fence, washed the car,
Pruned the roses, cut the hedges,
Swept up leaves from near and far.

Wise men constantly remind us,
Sunday is the day of rest,
So I'll sit down in the garden,
And do as they suggest.

As I close my eyes to have a nap,
Perhaps for just an hour –
I hear this noisy bumblebee
Buzz, buzzing round a flower.

A motorbike roars up the lane,
A horse comes trotting down,
A noisy plane flies overhead
Making circuits round the town.

Next door the motor mower
Marches up and down the grass,
Their screaming kid has fallen
And landed on his ass!

A jet plane whines across the sky,
Where bound I do not care,
The countryside is not quiet,
As I rest here in my chair.

Above the noise of planes and cars,
The sound that bothers me,
Is not the mower, kids, nor bikes
It's that noisy, buzzing bee!

CRISIS IN TOYLAND – 1

Things look bad in Toyland
About as bad as bad can be
And all because poor Santa's sleigh
Has failed the MOT,
The North Pole Sleigh Garage
Is searching hard to see
If they can help, but warn him
They can give no guarantee.

Now most everyone is trying
To find the needed parts
So lots and lots of children
Will not get broken hearts.
The reindeer all were harnessed
The toys were almost packed
Santa's policemen stood nearby
In case he got hi-jacked.

Santa's merry band of helpers
Worked hard both night and day
Wrapping toys and presents
To load on Santa's sleigh
But not until the sleigh was packed
Just as high as they could go
Santa notice it was broken
And sinking deeply in the snow.

The repair manager, (Sleighs) -
Was quickly on the scene
His verdict was not as helpful
As they hoped it might have been.
Out came the service manual
"Last service? – Let me see, -
Yes, here we are", he pointed out
"It was done in ninety three!"

They turned the reindeer out to graze
And unloaded all the toys
So kids you must be patient -
This means girls as well as boys,
Poor Santa's sad about the sleigh
He is really far from merry -
Thinking of the pies he'll miss-
And all that lovely sherry!

*

THE LONELINESS

The loneliness of marriage
Is always hard to bear.
Especially when the one you wed
No longer seems to care.

The flames of love that glowed so bright
Are smouldering ashes in the night
The vows we made not long ago
Have melted like the April snow.

I wonder where it all went wrong
What were the basic facts?
That induced my love to run away
The day I bought the axe!

CRISIS IN TOYLAND – II

Now things were bad in Toyland
About as bad as bad could be
All because poor Santa's sleigh
Had failed it's M.O.T.
When Tom, the salesman, heard the news
About poor Santa's trouble
He took a new sleigh out of stock
And rushed round at the double!

"Santa, let me show you why
We call this sleigh the Rocket –
Many extras have been added
You will not be out of pocket!"
Tom showered praise upon the sleigh
"It was the very latest -
And comes with many special features
Gee – this model is the greatest!"

"This new sleigh really looks smart
In scarlet trimmed with gold!
Note the really super heater
Just in case your toes get cold!
A reclining seat with head rest,
Yet another point I'll mention -
Guaranteed for three whole years!
Before it needs attention!"

"Of course the power steering -
Makes it easier to park.
You will be glad of extra head-lights
When you are driving in the dark.

There is another great advantage!
Reindeer you will not need
Think of all the cash you'll save
On hay, on oats, and feed!"

Then a message came for Santa
The needed parts were found
Santa's sleigh can be repaired
And Santa will be round.
He will harness up his reindeer
Load the sleigh high, high with toys
Then Santa will start on his way
So be good, good girls and boys!

*

O'REILLY

O'Reilly's delighted –not a touch of remorse
A gypsy lad has sold him a two-legged horse
T's a cert for the Derby – he will be ever so rich!
(The Zoo is offering a reward for a missing ostrich)

*

THE OLD SCHOOL HOUSE

The old school house burned down today,
While the children were at play
The fire brigade arrived too late
The postman delivers just after eight!

ODE TO A BAKED BEAN (UNFINISHED)

Oh wonder bean, oh mighty bean,
What a magical wind machine!
Oh wonder bean, oh noble bean,
So often heard but never seen!

Oh wonder bean, oh naughty bean,
Flatulence maker most obscene,
Oh wonder bean, oh vulgar bean,
Sometimes vapid, sometimes mean!

Oh wonder bean, oh stentorian bean,
Oh wonder bean, oh learned bean,
So turbulent and boisterous!
You converse in many voices!

Oh furtive bean, oh eruptive bean
There is no mystery where you have been
Those tummy gases played their part
So once again it's time to....!

Nudge, nudge, rumour, rumour,
Subject of much childish humour,
In classrooms full of girls or boys,
Not one admits who made the noise!

The politician swore it was not his intent
When he sat down in parliament!
The Speaker called for "Order! Please!
Do suppress retorts like these!

The church was quiet - all were listening
When you interrupted today's christening,
And later round the festive table
You sure embarrassed Auntie Mabel!

At weddings you harass nervous brides
By talking out of their backsides
Just as the ceremony is about to start
You blurt out a voluptuous....!

But wonder bean, oh redolent bean
So flavourful bean, so sumptuous bean
I relish, I savour you the most
Served hot and tasty on my toast!

*

PEGASUS MOOSE

As Pegasus Moose flew slowly by,
A hunter shot him from the sky,
Sad to say they both are dead!
The moose landed on the hunter's head!

APPOINTMENTS

Appointments, appointments, the amiable receptionists try
With patience, to help our patients, who can be difficult to satisfy.
Every patient with a problem wants someone to understand -
Someone they can rely on, and provide a healing hand.

So, patients seek help, with eager unction
Hoping to improve some body function.
Impatient, they sit waiting, skipping idly through
Accumulated magazines the way folk seem to do.

Those with complaints of all descriptions
Depart content with their prescriptions,
Children playing with the toys
Break the silence with their noise!

The Weston-Smythes and Spencer-Flloyds?
(In confidence, -- concerns -- haemorrhoids.)
But droll Sid Jones and his brother Giles
Have come for help about their piles.

Patients come and patients go
Still we tarry row on row.
The teenage youth blushes for all to see
When summoned by his lady D!

The T-Shirted girl simpering with delight
Confides to her friend about last night.
Then I hear someone behind me sneeze -
And hope it is not some dread disease.

The old folk go shuffling slowly by
On legs that once were strong and spry –
Then suddenly - we are down to three –!
First him, then her, and then it's ME!

Appointments, appointments, staff forever trying -
Being patient, helping patients can be very satisfying.
When you are feeling rotten, imagining dread complaints,
We will do our best to help but we are very short on saints!

*

MOM'S OLD WATCH

Mom's old watch lies in the drawer
Been there thirty years and a little bit more
An everyday watch, it is not unique
In a few more years it will be classed antigue
Antique or not it will just have to stay
I simply cannot bear to give Mom's watch away!

*

PASSPORT PHOTOS

Passport photos tell the tale,
Starting as a young aspiring male
Sometimes a leader on the trail
Seeking, searching for the Grail
Now the photo that you see
Shows an old man just like me!

THE RABBIT'S LAMENT

Why did you call me Romeo?
I would really like to know
I much prefer a stronger name
Like Mike or Bruce or Joe!
You must admit some names are good
That some names can be funny
But Romeo is not a name I'd give
To rabbit, hare or bunny!

Hopping down the road one day
I met a doe called Alice
She was sweet and oh so fair -
She lived down by the palace.
She spurned my letters and my love
She married Beauregard
He was a knave, a bounder
And I took it very hard.

The note she sent before she wed
Was brief and to the point-
There was no way her father
Would let a Romeo near the joint!
My friends who live in Scotland
Are nearly all called Bruce
They eat a lot of porridge
But that's really no excuse.

There are many other cousins
Whose names I can recall
Like Roger, Ronald, Robert,
Peter, Teddy, Tom, and Paul.
So one day, when I'm older,
I'll change my name to Troy
And when the lady bunnies chase me -
Oh boy! Oh Boy! OH BOY!

SHE

Very much against her wishes
She was forever washing dishes,

She was always washing clothes
And much more goodness knows!

One day she thought enough's enough
To hell with all this housework stuff!

So she who had been a constant wife
Decided there were better things in life!

Just then a circus happened by
She decided to give their life a try-

So working hard to much acclaim
A bareback rider she became!

Then with almost consummate ease
Became adept on the high trapeze!

Twice each day the crowds enthral
Now she is the human cannonball!

Her fame for daring has simply soared
She is famous now and never bored!

But when she is blue her greatest wish is
To help in the kitchen washing dishes!

THE BLOOD LADIES

Blood, blood, they keep taking your blood.
And they do not seem to mind if it's thin or like mud!

You wonder how brave those departing have been -
As they hurry away looking pale shades of green!

Your number is called and they welcome you in
"Sit down, roll up your sleeve so I can begin -"

"There's no need to make faces - the needle is sharp
And simply no reason for you to fidget or carp!"

"We are just taking a sample to check your O.K.
Oh, do stop your wriggling or we will be here all day!"

"That's it, all finished! - was it such a disaster?
You press on the swab while I fix the plaster!"

"There was no reason to worry - we've got the knowledge
We're all graduates (with honours) from Dracula College!"

POOR COUSIN JOE

We buried Cousin Joe today
Beneath the apple tree,
(The one he started climbing)
When he was only three.

Now in his teens he sure went wrong,
He started robbing banks,
He stole lots and lots of money -
And never once said "Thanks".

Rustling cattle was his hobby,
Robbing trains he said was fun,
He told a naughty bar room girl
She was his number one.

When she discovered he was cheating,
She claimed the big reward,
They hung Cousin Joe from the tree,
Suspended by a cord!

Poor Cousin Joe now lies beneath,
The tree with apples green,
The tree Mom requested he chop down
When he was just fifteen.

And now throughout the summer,
We watch these apples grow
When folk ask "What fertilizer?"
We just say "Cousin Joe!"

AIRLINES

You really should be suspicious
About flying with Air Maritius,

The planes I hear are quite fantastic
Powered by old knicker elastic.

All repairs are swiftly made
With bailing twine and old Band-aid

Flying o'er the Indian Ocean
Will surely need so much devotion

You may or may not give a hoot
If they do not provide a parachute

Or fly a plane patched up with mastic,
Built with care from recycled plastic

When you fly your Hawk about the sky
Say "Gee, what a lucky guy am I".

You know that British is the best
So fly BA and skip the rest!

THE WAITING GAME

We sit in silence waiting,
Our brave backs against the wall,
We wait anxiously in silence,
Listening for the nurse's call.

Number One did not take very long,
Number Two about the same,
Number Three has been in for ages,
As we play this waiting game.

Four was quickly in, and out,
But five was not so fast,
Now six are still ahead of me -
Thank goodness I'm not last!

So ever hopeful I'm still waiting -
Even hide my disappointment,
As Nurse calls out for "William Brown?"
(He's one with an appointment!)

And as I wait, I ponder -
Just how long William Brown will be.
Then count again how many
Are still ahead of me!

At last, at last! my turn has come,
I hear Nurse kindly say,
"Roll up your sleeve, this won't take long -
They want a pint today!"

WILLIE MCKENZIE

Young Willie McKenzie from Achnasheen
Was the brawniest Scotsman you've ever seen
Tall as the oak, twice as strong as an ox.
Young Will' was the bravest of all of the Jocks!

All through the highlands his fame grew and grew
Soon across Scotland so everyone knew
Young Willie McKenzie wud na'e denied
As he searched for the woman to be at his side!

He trod many a glen, he strode many a moor
He met girls that were rich, girls that were poor
But none of the lassies Young Willie could find
Were a patch of the lass Will had in his mind!

Now Morag McQueen with her flowing red hair
Thought she and Young Willie would make a great pair
So straightaway she headed for yon Achnasheen
To meet with the brawniest man she'd ever seen!

Her disappointment was bitter as she later recalled
She simply could na'e marry a man that was bald
Young Willie may have just turned twenty-five
But he'd been bald as a boulder since he was just five!

Now Morag McQueen with her long flowing hair
Was na'e sort of lass to give up in despair
She made an offer - if all folk were shaved bald
And that is the way her problem was solved!

Then right across Scotland for just half a shilling
All folk went bald, for na'e Scot was unwilling!
Now Morag McQueen dwells in yon Achnasheen
With the bonniest bairns that you've ever seen!

They're bald of course for all Scots were willing
To have their heads shaved for just half a shilling!
So when in your journey you reach Achnasheen
Your head will be shaved, thanks to Morag McQueen!

*

ONE BY ONE

One by one they have slipped away -
Old friends and loves of yesterday.
Where they have gone they did not say
I miss those friends of yesterday!

Where they have gone it is hard to tell -
Perhaps to heaven, perhaps to hell.
Wherever they are I wish them well
Especially those who have gone to hell!

AUNTIE BELLA

So dear Auntie Bella has gone on her way
(And not up to heaven), so the gossips all say
Malicious stories for years have been told
Of naughty Aunt Bella and her heart of gold.

Stories true or false I cannot say,
I clearly remember what I saw that day -
Eight shiny black horses drew her coffin along
Behind came a cortege of men two miles long!

I saw five kings and three presidents
They all bowed their heads in deep reverence
Billionaires, millionaires came to be seen
Each arrived in his flash limousine

The railway supplied ten special trains
The airline chartered many extra planes
Cheeky Bella would have been so proud
She always attracted men by the crowd!

Men who had known from the very start
The way to win the lovely Bella's heart
Dear Bella loved expensive things
Rolex watches, diamond rings,

Long fur coats of mink or sable
The best horse in the top racing stable
A private jet plane for her pleasure
A Rolls-Royce car for her to treasure!

Six times she married men with cash
Men who folk might say were rash,
But men that could not stand the pace
To heaven went with a smiley face.

All men found sweet Belle a great attraction
In her love all men found satisfaction
Romantic men longing to be her friends
Would know a large diamond never offends!

As wise Aunt Bella's fortune grew and grew
Her family pondered whom she would leave her lucre to?
To stop them arguing, bickering, having spats
Bella left all her millions to a home for stray cats!

Now as sweet Bella floats by on a fluffy white cloud
Men still doff their hats and feel ever so proud
Each hoping when he reaches the Pearly Gate
The heavenly pleasures of kind Bella await!

*

SWEET MEMORIES

Sweet memories recalled in rhyme
Memories worn thin by time
The ashes of those early fires
Puppy love, teenage desires
All those plans - all those wishes
Lie scattered now - like broken dishes!

PRAIRIE SWEETHEART

Way out on the prairie
Where the setting suns a'glowing
Lives a maiden sweet and fair
A gal that's well worth knowing.

She dances like a demon
And she kisses very well
I'm hoping one day we will wed
But time alone will tell.

As the evening sun is sinking
And you a'riding by her side
Oh the pleasure a'waiting for you
On this prairie vast and wide.

The harvest moon shines like gold
The stars are big and bright
Everything is wonderful
As you ride into the night

*

THE TUTOR

His tutor thought it was not fair
A dolt like him could, from the air,
Plucking the correct words to rhyme,
Compile sweet verses every time!
And compose with consummate ease.
In Russian, Norwegian and Chinese!

DOLORES

Where do I begin, where do I start?
This tale of Dolores, a nudist at heart,

A Mexican beauty was lovely Dolores-
A really high kicker as she danced in the chorus!

She loved to strip naked and lie in the sun,
Play netball or tennis or simply have fun!

She once loved a sailor: so my uncle did say,
Who played happy families at home and away,

He suggested Dolores could make a good wage,
(Lap dancing had become the latest new rage,)

Being a nudist was fine on days that are sunny,
But strippers he knew made lots of money!

Soon Dolores was famous –she had a new twist
A stripper for cash and a happy nudist!

One night a millionaire gave her the wink
He proposed. They eloped and were wed in a blink,

They are living in Texas where every male knows,
The erotic way Dolores slips out of her clothes.

CHILDHOOD MEMORIES OF THE PRAIRIES

Freight trains calling in the summer night
Swooping owls in silent flight
Haultain School with all the mystery
Of learning maths and early history
Wooden sidewalks, and streetcars
The smell of smoke from Dad's cigars.

To Sunday school with parted hair
Your all dressed up – "Now do take care -
Sing the right words to each song
Not the ones you know are wrong,
Today the vicar is coming to tea
So try not to embarrass me!"

Roving Indians camped nearby
Teepees dark against the sky
The buffalo hunters of long ago
Rejected now with no place to go
Thunderstorms, the crack of lightening
Rainbows when the skies are brightening.

Memories of a childhood spent
Of days that came, the years that went
The soft caressing summer breeze
Leaves rustling on the shimmering trees
Bright morning sun at it's shiny best
Until sinking golden in the West.

THE ADJECTIVES' REVENGE

Old Grand-dad narrates many stories and tales
Of his ancient buddies who went off the rails!
Cruel men who were evil; wicked, badder than bad,
Vile sort of thugs who would steal, pinch all you had!

There was big, large, massive, huge, arrogant, blustering Ed Morse
Who caught a wicked, depraved, dishonest villain stealing his horse!
It was gruff, surly, rude, ungracious, grumpy Three Finger Bob Pope.
The sheriff said, "I presume, suppose, believe, this man's due for the rope!"

So they hung, suspended, dangled him from a stout, strong cord.
That was the finish, end, termination of Bob who is now with his Lord.
Then there was flashy, showy, ostentatious Patrick O'Kelly Mulroon,
Who married stout, portly, chubby, bonny, redheaded Rosie Calhoun!

As time went, proceeded, continually moving, blundering on,
They had seven plump, cheerful, happy children, all christened John!
"Shorty" McDonald was a tall, lofty, towering, incredible man,
Who drank strong, potent, rye whisky all day from a can!

He married a pigheaded, stubborn, obstinate, contrary, teetotal lass
Now "Shorty" drinks, swallows, guaffs, imbibes only lemonade in his glass!
His best friend was nefarious, disreputable, detestable, wicked Sam Cook
A rustler, a swindler, embezzler, kleptomaniac, and crook!

They all have departed, left, scampered, vamoosed or high tailed it away
As Grand-dad recounts, recites and regales us with his stories all day!

THE WHISTLERS

At school I knew a girl called Rose
She could whistle through her nose

Her cousin's name was Alice Hutton
She whistled through her tummy button

Her father who could be very coarse
Made noises louder than the milkman's horse

It is not for you to think or care
Why her father was quite full of air

But worst of all was Auntie Nellie
Silent, strong and very smelly

And then I met a girl called Annie
Now she really could whistle!

*

LUCREZIA

A reservoir of emotions
A barrel of devotions
A pail of notions
A cup of lotions
A draught of potions

SHE WAS SWEET AND SHE WAS FAIR

He flew jets across the sky
She worked in the pub nearby

Where they met I cannot say
For this might give the game away

Oh she was sweet and she was fair
(And wore expensive underwear)

Now he had never known such bliss
When she responded to his kiss

He said he loved her and caressed her
Spoke of love and then undressed here

I promised I would never tell
About that night he said went well

I have said enough I'll say no more
I promised, that's what friends are for.

He is married now to someone who
Would castrate him if she knew!

*

HAND-IN-HAND

Hand in hand along the shore
We pledged our love forevermore
But that was many years ago –
Now was it Jean or Jane or Flo!

OUR CAPTAIN

Our Captain wrote to her every day,
We wondered what he found to say,

Been over three years since we departed
A thousand letters since he started.

Pledges of love, words of devotion?
So many lines penned with emotion.

A billet d'amour romantizing?
Perhaps a billet doux fanaticising?

The delayed post arrived today
Mail from four thousand miles away

Letters from home for every one
But for our Captain there was just one

When he read what the letter contained
The Captain scowled – he sure looked pained

Brief, written in a flowery hand –
" I hope that you will understand,

The postman came daily with your letter
We got to know each other better.

Love blossomed, - love grew strong,
Sorry, but I have been waiting too long.

Now there is a new man in my life
The postman proposed - I am now his wife.

I waited three years, - now my new love calls –
We are on our honeymoon at Niagara Falls!"

THE PROBATION OFFICER

The probation officer sat in his chair,
And thought very hard of the world out there,
He though such a thought, such a thought, thought he,
Now if the world was just perfect, as perfect could be -
Why there would be no call for a man like me.
He remembered his training, the things he had learned,
How to cope with the people, the people life spurned,
Then he smiled such a smile, such a smile, smiled he -
For this world is not perfect and never will be.
Then went on with his work - what a lucky man he!

*

SMOKY

Smoky was hunting cat
Killing this and killing that
Now Smoky's grown old and fat.

Smoky's hunting days are done
While Smoky dozes in the sun -
The blackbirds pluck his fur for fun!

THE COLOUR OF LOVE

Bright blue today
Dove grey tomorrow
Rose red for love
Jet black for sorrow

Saffron gold hair
Maize yellow flowers
Soft amber moons
Fresh rainbow showers

Cherry red lips
Smiling green eyes
Corn coloured freckles
Azure blue skies

Blushing pink cheeks
Auburn brown tresses
The colour of love?
I'll give you three guesses!

THE POTMAN'S TALE

It were a warm summer evening with a gold setting sun
When I were a lad back in 1651
These riders rode up to seeking shelter you see
One handsome lady grinned a sweet smile to me
"Boy - look well to my mare, we sure had to dash!"
It were then that I glimpsed she had a moustache!
Well, I stabled the mare, fed her corn and sweet hay.
Then I asked Old Will Tupper what he had to say
The only moustached lady Will could remember
Be when the circus came by two year last September!
I heard my name called by my master who said -
"Jonas, take care as you empty the pots under each bed.
In a five star hostel every thing must be right
Your job is to empty the pots through the night!"
Come midnight, the sound of music I heard
I told the housekeeper and she replied "That's absurd!
Some one's filling their pot and it's ever so clear
It's only chamber music you are likely to hear!
With ten travellers asleep full of good Sussex ale
They will fill every pot, best you fetch a large pail!"
Chamber music I did hear all through the night
Thrice! Three times! I emptied every pisspot in sight!
The lady with the moustache, she sure slept a lot
Except when she woke to fill up her pot!
At first light of day, she roused from her slumber,
A sword by her side, dressed in a blue velvet number
A long feathered hat and embroidered handbag
Who ever would think it were a man wearing drag

Then they riders be gone and come later in day
Will said it were King, he reasoned this way -
Only King would have his own pot to pee
Adorned with three crowns and "C" for Charlie!

History records King Charles kept the royal pot under his bed
And used it the morning they chopped off his head!

*

Remembering Max and Jemma

THE DAY WE RODE TO HEAVEN

One bright new August morning we trotted down the lane
The world refreshed and sparkling after early dawning rain.

On keen and willing horses we soon reached the bridleway
Through the gate, across the field, then upwards on our way.

The sky was blue, the flax was blue, the flowers stirrup high.
The flax stretched out before us until it touched the sky.

As we cantered ever upwards no horizon could we see,
We were riding up to heaven, riding to eternity!

SASKATCHEWAN

The sky was blue as I remember
From January through to late December
Across the prairie we would roam
Yet never going far from home
For home was where our friends would meet
At eight, six, five on Lindsay Street.

Waking on a bright new winter morning
With deep shining snow all things adorning
Snow that crunched beneath our feet
The games that made our days complete
Building snowmen, snowball fights
The wonder of the Northern Lights.

The warmth of spring, the melting snow
The hated mess of sticky gumbo
The sound of wild birds flying high
Skeins of geese across the sky
Throughout the day, all through the night
We saw and heard this annual sight.

Playful kids with barking dogs
The croaking of a thousand frogs
Freight trains moan from far away
To tell us they are on their way
Wooden sidewalks, the old streetcars
The smell of smoke from cheap cigars.

The summer storms were wild and loud
The roar of thunder, black purple cloud
Flashing lightning, pouring rain
Rainbows to warm your heart again
Then without a worry, without a care
We ran and played most everywhere.

In our outside toilet standing forlorn
The Leader Post in squares was torn
Sometimes a page or two we'd spare
(Of the girls displaying underwear)
Eatons' treasures – Simpson's too
Magic worlds that we so seldom knew.

On Sundays pancakes Dad would make
While Mum excelled at ginger cake
Remember how young Les was flustered
When Mum spiked the cake with real hot mustard.
Then off to school with all the misery
Of learning maths and ancient history.

Early morning sun, the noonday heat
The ripening of the golden wheat
Necessary chores were always done
In winter's cold and summer's sun
The wood-burning stove we loved to hate
Bathwater heating on the grate
Three in the tub –then off to sleep
With a prayer to God our souls to keep.

*

YOUNG GERALDINE

Young Geraldine Potter couldn't wait –
So went behind the garden gate
A nettle stung her little tookus
So now before she squats – she lookus.

THE MAGIC GARDEN

There is magic in the garden,
When the buds begin to show,
One by one they will appear
Above the melting snow.

The sudden flush of flowers,
To welcome every spring,
The bright new splash of colour
The joy that blossoms bring.

In the magic of a garden,
Bees hum for many hours,
While butterflies take their ease
Upon the willing flowers.

In the beauty of a garden,
So much pleasure waits for you,
There is magic of a garden
To enjoy the summer through.

The slugs may eat your lettuce
The birds eat all your seeds
The pigeons peck your cabbage
Yet ignore the host of weeds.

It is tragic in the garden
As seedlings start to grow
Large hungry snails appear
And devour them row by row.

Next season come what may
We will try to get it right
To create the magic garden
About which the poets write!

BUTTERFLY (U A E I O U)

Flutter by butterfly, flutter by do
Sometimes you are alone
Sometimes there are two!

Flatter by batterfly flatter by please
You dance over the bushes
And up through the trees!

Fletter by betterfly fletter by too
You are very lovely
So small and so blue!

Flitter by bitterfly flitter by past
Sometimes you are first
Sometimes you are last!

Flotter by botterfly flotter by soon
When I am asleep
Will you fly to the moon?

Flutter by butterfly flutterby do
I think butterfly
Is the right name for you!

*

TOMMY SMITH

"Tommy Smith, oh me, oh my!
Who hit you with a custard pie?
It wasn't me - it wasn't I
Fingers crossed, I tell a lie."

WOODY

Oh what a dog was our Jack Russell,
Small, but strong, and full of muscle
Tugging ropes or chasing rats,
He kept the garden free of cats.

But kind and gentle, sweet as May
W hen Chris and Cassie came to stay.
Cadger of biscuits, lover of stew
Begging to eat the same as you.

Your favourite armchair was his choice
He would grumble in his lowest voice
Then jumping down, the clever chap
Would leap back upon your lap.

Cuddled beside you in your chair
His friendly warmth was yours to share
At night he loved to snuggle down
And hide beneath your eiderdown.

Black button nose exposed for air
He kept so still while hiding there,
Early mornings he would fly
Barking at the dustbin guy.

He'd chase the postman without fail
When he came delivering mail,
The paperboy on his squeaking bike
Was someone else he did not like.

Barking, snarling till they had gone
Then back to bed to slumber on,
And now he's gone where good dogs go
The pal we loved and still miss so.

MEDICATION

Each day I take a clutch of pills
Prescribed to control my several ills!

The Consultant thought it might be wise
To chew one pill before I rise!

He suggested times throughout the day -
That I keep to the schedule come what may!

Four pills, as directed, before eating food
Doctor maintains they are doing me good!

Then one hour later I swallow two more
Two tablets at twelve, repeat dose at four!

Take two more at seven, another at ten
Come the next morning I start over again!

All taken with water – a full glass of course
No wonder these days I pee like a horse!

YEARNING

I really must stop - stop going on
But I am homesick for Saskatchewan
Where twinkling stars shine so bright
A big yellow moon spread it's light.

The warm Chinook, the croaking frogs
Paddling kids and muddy dogs
Melt water running everywhere
We played all day without a care.

Day and night, the constant sound
Of honking geese all northward bound
The joy of spring, the passing showers
Sudden storms that last for hours.

The growl of thunder rolling by
Flashing lightening across the sky
The summer sun, the golden grain
The mournful whistle of a train.

The icy winds of winter blow
Heralding frosts and then the snow
Now your world is gleaming white
Time to sleigh and snowball fight.

The crunch of footsteps in the snow
As homeward on our way we go.
Dark winter nights the sky's a treasure
With far more stars than you can measure.

After Christmas the New Year will bring
The magic of another spring.
Those happy days of long ago
Wherever did my lifetime go?

It's time to stop, best not keep on
About the joys of Saskatchewan
But forever in my heart will be
This yearning for that wide prairie.

*

QUESTIONS

What happened to the girl I wed
Sleeping now in her lover's bed
The wife I spent those years adoring -
I expect he puts up with her snoring!

What happened to the girl I knew
Who looked so lovely dressed in blue
She looked even better in the nude
Say no more - she was so prude!

SEPTIMUS JONES

This poem is about old Septimus Jones
Who loved to collect odd animal bones,
With sixteen of this and eleven of that
He created a goat and a seven tailed cat.

Now he has a friend called Sylvester Doo
Who always was keen to start his own zoo
He crossed a red hen with an green plastic mac
And so got a bird with a waterproof back.

He worked and he struggled for many a day
Then happily Sylvester discovered a way
Of crossing a cow, a horse and a moose
He decided to call the baby a Choose!

The press and the T.V. then got real agitated
When they saw just what Old Syl had created
He showed them the Choose and now the world knows
They come in three colours and have a long nose.

Then he discovered a fish that could fly
And hairy blue spider with a very big eye
There is a clever old monkey with so many tricks
And a hippo that juggles all day with some bricks.

A tiger with spots that just loves to croon
While a chimp plays a trumpet that is sure out of tune
Plus an old circus horse that is yellow and red
His cleverest trick is to stand on his head.

Now Septimus Jones owned a cat and a dog
An old yellow goat and a very green frog
He went to a party - the frog won first prize
A bucket of fish and seven old pies.

He had a young sister – she was called Abigail
Who decided to ride round the world on a snail.
She rode across France and halfway across Spain
Then the snail ran away so she came home again.

Next year she told us that her greatest wish
Was to ride round the world on the back of a fish,
But somewhere of China she slipped of it's tail
So our daring young lady ended up on a whale.

Septimus Jones has a friend who likes sheep
He counts them each night before going to sleep
That is except Sundays when just for a laugh
He counts all the spots on his neighbour's giraffe.

Now Septimus Jones and Sylvester Doo
And of course not forgetting young Abigail too
All send their best wishes and hope you will rhyme
A last line for this poem - they've run out of time.

THE WATERPROOF HEN

Remember I told you a story
The one about Sylvester Doo
A really strange kind of fellow
Who was keen to start his own zoo.

It all began with a waterproof hen
And a strange kind of thing called a Choose
Now he has added a real roaring lion
Plus a singing and dancing mongoose.

There's a wonderful zebra with stripes
Stripes that simply run the wrong way
A winking and blinking blue owl
That just keeps on hooting all day.

The camel with three humps is super
So much better than having just two
The children just love to ride him
When they come to visit the zoo.

He bought a green and red elephant
It came on a ship from Bombay
But the incessant rain in old England
Simply washed all the colours away.

A friend gave him two very young rabbits
(And you know what young bunnies do)
Now when he got around to count them
There were over a hundred and two.

There is a tortoise that roars like a lion
And a donkey that croaks like a frog
A sparrow that sings Yankee Doodle
And a piglet that barks like a dog.

There is also a little grey field mouse
The mouse just adored eating cheese
Then it grew a long tail that is curly
And waves to and fro in the breeze.

There is also a house full of monkeys
Young children love them the most
There are blue ones, green ones and red ones.
And one that just sits on a post.

So when it comes round to the weekend
The very best thing you can do
Is be kind to your Mum and your Daddy
And let them take you to the zoo.

*

A PLEA FOR LARGER DUSTBINS

Driving along the country roads
Down lanes and over ridges
You see dumped on every lay-by
Wantonly discarded fridges

Perhaps the local councils
Renowned for many sins
Could keep countryside tidier
By providing larger bins!

MEMORIES AND THINGS

Sometimes I'm happy,
Sometimes I'm sad
When ever I meet you
I'm happy and glad!

Then I remember
Why we drifted apart,
The quite callous way
You broke my heart!

This makes me unhappy
So miserable and sad
I think of my new love
And begin to feel glad!

I think of the happiness
That my new love brings
Perhaps it is best we forget
Old memories and things!

*

WORDS

Words for love
Words for beauty
Words for devotion
Words for duty
Words that say my heart is true
Words to say I do love you!

THE SUSSEX DOWNS

I walk along the Sussex Downs
Beneath a clear blue sky
The shining, sparkling sea below
Where lazy seagulls fly.

At night the moon gleams on the sea
The sky is full of stars
While all along the Downs I see
The glow of burning cars.

And in the newness of the morning
As you drive across the bridges
You see where vandals dump
Old mattresses and fridges.

Is it only on the Sussex Downs,
Where folks are dense or bitter?
If they would use some common sense
And take home their awful litter!

Then all along the Sussex Downs
Where lazy seagulls fly
The Downs will look a better place
For folk like you and I!

RAIN ON MONDAYS

Rain on Mondays? Of course its' true!
Rain on Monday means the next day too!
Most Wednesdays we get hail or sleet
With gales that sweep us off our feet!
Thursday's rain goes on for hours
When it stops, down come the showers!
Fridays, Saturdays and even Sundays! -
Just when we hope to have some fun days,
Those smiling weather folk explain
The weekend forecast is for rain! -
They quote from records long years ago,
About the rain, the winds and snow,
If rain and sleet fall through September
We may get sunshine by December!

P.S.

And when it stops raining they think you should know
We will wake up next morning under a blanket of snow

The a/m poem is sponsored by the Nevaleekie Umbrella
and Rubber Boot Company.
Nevaleekie Rubber Boots and Umbrellas are
available from selected stores.
Sizes 3 to 18.
"If your steps are short and squeaky we know you're wearing Nevaleekie".

A NIGHT OUT WITH THE BOYS

A young man I know just phoned to say -
He was not feeling well today.
His stomach pained, so did his head,
He could not get to sleep in bed.

His other parts were aching too,
Ten times he'd hurried to the loo,
And every time he had to scurry,
Just one of the joys of eating curry.

He'd spewed up here, he'd thrown up there,
Emitted foul smells in the air,
Rank odours from the kitchen sink
It's dreadful how his house does stink!

To belch all day and puke all night
To puke, (n, pewk,) cannot be right.
Did the meal you ate taste yummy
Leave a warm glow in your tummy?

Will this morbid excavation
Live up to your expectation?
Yes, diarrhea is a horrid plight,
And can take away your appetite.

Next time I hope you take more care -
Be sure to clean up everywhere.
So feeling as you say you do,
Perhaps you best stay on the loo!

For Chris – November 2001

NORWEGIAN GIRLS

Norwegian girls are tall and fair
With lovely eyes and golden hair.

Norwegian girls just ooze with charms
And long to hold you in their arms.

Norwegian girls are loving, thrilling -
You will meet one that's very willing.

Ingrid is sweet as folding money
Olga bathes in wild bee's honey.

Sonja will dance till the sun rises
Katja's the one who loves surprises.

Affectionate girls with golden hair
Have younger sisters everywhere.

And all these girls with golden tresses
Are slim and tall and fill their dresses.

The secret when you get to Norway?
Best of your luck and play it your way.

BY APPOINTMENT

The letter from the Palace read
I am inviting you to tea,
And if you would like to bring a friend
That is quite all right with me.

Now Billy's friend was Jimmy Brown
A naughty sort of child.
Sometimes good and sometimes bad
But mostly very wild.

They rehearsed their please and thank-you's
Till they knew them off by heart,
But when they bowed before the Queen
Boy did Jimmy fart!

The noise echoed round the palace
Through every room and bower,
The Queen sent for the royal guard -
They locked Jimmy in the tower!

They shipped him to Australia
Where cabbage plants abound,
Eating greens and swilling lager
He learned to make a mournful sound.

Now Jim mimes tuba with his band -
(Not to everyone's enjoyment)
But both the odorous fragrance and his tunes
Are NOT backed by "Royal Appointment."

WEATHER GIRL

Oh weather girl, dear weather girl,
You smile and look so smart,
Then forecast the sort of weather
That would break a sailor's heart!

Oh weather girl, wise weather girl,
With complex charts you show
Gales bringing stormy weather,
Then rain, then sleet, then snow!

Oh weather girl, sweet weather girl,
You point out in Fahrenheit,
That tomorrow will be warmer
But there will be frost tonight!

Oh weather girl, kind weather girl,
Now you have had your fun,
Please press your magic button
And bring back the summer sun!

*

TOM

Tom eats potato crisps in bed
His wife loves eating crusty bread
Friday night they like the most
They do enjoy baked beans on toast!
And if the wind blows in the night
They cuddle up and hold on tight!

SUDDEN GLIMPSE

A sudden glimpse of your smiling face -
And my heart skips to another time and place.

To another girl who looks like you
Comely, tender, winsome, true.

I recall the love we found that day
In my homeland far away.

Such happiness - what love divine -
She gave her heart and I gave mine.

Strawberry lips so sweet so tender
A thousand kisses I remember.

I close my eyes, I see her there
With laughing eyes and golden hair.

We wandered slowly hand in hand
Through a teen-age wonderland.

Never thinking that one day
A war would take me far away.

In my heart you have always been -
Will be forever, sweet sixteen.

My love your smile will always be
The treasure of the world to me.

MOLLY MCAULLY

I have an aunt - her name is Molly,
She's such great fun and always jolly,

Molly wed a sailor named McAully,
Named after his rich granddad "Ollie",

Now Molly is Mrs Molly McAully,
She is very proud of her sister Holly!

Molly McAully has a collie named Dolly,
Bought from a vet, surname of Wally,

Ollie sailed home with his pet parrot Polly,
Polly will swear, then say "gosh-oh-golly"!

Dolly the collie, swallowed poor Polly,
So Molly McAully whacked him with her brolly!

Without Polly, Ollie is quite melancholy
But Molly is pleased with her talking collie!

*

SNIPPETS OF VERSE

A sailor boy called Appleby
Had beans for breakfast, lunch and tea
Foul winds have blown him out to sea
Lonely Johnny Appleby.

JOSEF KLOPPENHIEMER

Josef Kloppenhiemer was extremely clever
Terms: Strictly cash - no way never-never!

For babes he made cradles, cots and swings
For the elderly rocking chairs, coffins and things.

So Kloppenhiemer's Joinery succeeded
Making the wood goods all folk needed.

Yes, Kloppenhiemer was very wise
He built a motel way up in the skies.

Where folk could stop and meditate
Before they reached the Golden Gate.

Kloppenhiemer's Motel & Bargain Store
Stocks items needed in the great evermore,

Like haloes, harps, those sort of things
On special this month are "Angel's Wings"!

If on reaching the Golden Gates they say
Your destination is the other way.

Kloppenhiemer's Store is there as well
But picks and shovels are all they sell!

CIRCULARS

Circulars, circulars by the score
Are constantly delivered to my door

Each one claiming to be the best
Phone them now they will do the rest

I do not want a Swiss made clock
Or wear the latest fashion frock

Double-glazing we have had for years
There is no need to test my ears

Holidays – join our special cruise
Safari far away from winter blues

Cases of wine at knocked down prices
Jars of vitamins and varied spices

Special offers for weekend breaks
Guided tours to Italian lakes

Automatic this and automatic that
Phone their number and have a chat

Garden services by men who know
How to dig or lop or mow

A classic veranda or loft extension
Financial services for my attention

Today, if I order Christmas hampers
Because it's June I get free champers

I am simply not interested so please
Keep your junk and save the trees!

"ME?"

Compose a poem about a bird –
Now you are being quite absurd
And you think that I could pen
A few nice words about a wren?
Or good things concerning starlings? -
Folk hardly look on them as darlings!
Perhaps a rhyme about an eagle,
Are you sure such verse is legal?

Scores of books, with many chapters
Heap much praise upon the raptors.
It's possible to rhyme about a robin
Or wagtails and their constant bobbing.
Most country folk I do suppose
Tell tales about the rooks and crows,
A word or two about the finches
Would not take up too many inches.

And before the list begins to narrow
There must be some who love the sparrow
I trust folk do not think me rude
For not naming tits in multitude.
The skylarks fill the day with song
The blackbirds call and sing along
Now beyond the castle walls
A red necked pheasant calls and calls.

Thrushes banging snails on stones
The collar dove's incessant moans.
A sparrow hawk darts swiftly by
So quick to cover small birds fly
Buzzards circling, soaring high
Seagulls white against the sky
Passing crows with waving wings
The raucous bird that never sings

Swifts and swallows wheel and dart
Oh well, OK I'd better make a start
I know you will be happy when
I begin to write about the wren"

"Troglodytes, troglodytes, the wren –
Perhaps I can borrow paper and pen…"

WAITING MEMBERS ONLY

The Waiting Member as his name implies
May wait aeons before someone replies
So he attends in hope and expectation,
To do his bounden duty for the nation!

Imagine the anguish and the ballyhoo
When Columbus sailed west in one, four, nine, two,
The Waiting Member thinking he had been spurned
Waited three years before Columbus returned!

The Scots Waiting Member on Wellington's staff
Was happy-go-lucky, always good for a laugh
He cunna' care less, did not give ta'e hoots
But he'd na'e don the kilt wearing Wellington boots!

The brave Waiting Member at Custer's last stand
Stayed in the background with pistol in hand
When he rode into battle sadly history recalls
He lost not only his scalp but also his smalls!

Rejoice for Neil Armstrong, first man on the moon
Despair for the Member who waits alone in his room
To Neil went the glory that fills so many books
"But who ever mentions lonely George Snooks?"

Many Members it seems have waited in vain
But at least you are warm and out of the rain!
This may not bring glory, nor put gongs opon your chest
But whatever the duty give it your honest best!

THE HAPPY YEARS

The happy years where did they go?
Those happy years of long ago

The wonderful years of loves delights
The joyful days, the heavenly nights

Beneath the twinkling stars above
So rich in hope we fell in love

And for a while I do recall
Our love was the greatest love of all

Alas, perchance, some how it seems
We awoke from our happy dreams

And the love we thought would last forever?
Has blown away just like a feaver!

POETASTER - (A PETTY POET)

A petty poet I be
Hoping poetically

That I can rhyme
Thoughts so sublime

Of a love very real
A love I could feel

I was content
But off she went

No word of goodbye
She eloped with some guy

I've been downhearted
Since she departed

My verbal contention
Needs urgent attention

A poetaster hoping in time
A few lines will rhyme

Using second hand words
To beguile any birds

Willing to perch in my tree
And be poetized by me!

LINES

When teacher gave us lines to write
It was always with the warning
He wanted two hundred handwritten lines
On his desk by nine o'clock next morning!

He wrote strange words upon the board
Words like scholasticim, discombobulate,
Sophistory, isoperimetry, pusillanimous,
Philosophistical, discobolus and disambiguate.

I learned to spell each word correctly
As I wrote out my punishment
My only problem is
I wish I knew what they meant!

NON ESSENTIAL MUSINGS

"The streaker got the loudest cheer..."

"Not long now till spring is here!"

"I prefer the Alps in wintertime..."

"Yes, zetetic can be hard to rhyme..."

"Every day and twice on Sundays...!"

"The window cleaner comes on Mondays!"

"You can lead a horse to water..."

"Later he married Nero's daughter..."

"Folk say a dog is man's best friend..."

"Did they indicate when the world might end?"

"Once we went on holiday by train..."

"I think the forecast is for rain!"

"The smoked salmon should be good..."

"You cannot see the trees for the wood..."

"Icebergs keep melting come what may..."

"He thought our daffodils looked fine today!"

"Seventeen road humps slow the traffic..."

"Television should be more dramatic..."

"We went home with a bottle of wine..."

"The wood they used is knotty pine..."

"I simply try to cut back on the salt..."

"The Council swear they are not at fault..."

"The early bird should catch the worm..."

"I'm told the place would make you squirm..."

"She dislikes the fuss, the constant ruction..."

"I am fed up hearing about mass destruction..."

"When I asked how long she had been a member..."

"The school should open the end of September..."

"We drove down from London hoping see..."

"A privilege and pleasure for my wife and me..."

COUSIN EDWIN

My ingenious cousin Edwin Edgoose

Constantly invents things that are simply no use.

Like a three headed hammer and ready bent nails

Cricket stumps with securely glued bails.

His fish cakes with candles were not a success

And his tartan paint was really a mess.

His electric aeroplane became quite unstable

Dragging mile after mile of electric cable.

The underwater motorbike sadly went wrong

When the snorkel was over one hundred feet long.

But Edwin never gives up in despair

His latest idea is a one legged chair!

If that is not a success he is thinking ahead

Something to do with self - buttering bread!

CRISIS IN TOYLAND III

This is a hectic time in Toyland
Santa's busy rushing to and fro
He's filled lots and lots of orders
And there are plenty more to go!

Production has been going well
(Much better than expected)
Because most clever girls and boys
Posted early as suggested!

So Santa hurried in to town
To buy things he was needing
A police car requested him to stop
They arrested him for speeding!

They took Santa to the jailhouse
And locked him in a cell
Central heating - plus six reindeer
(Soon the jail began to smell!)

As the news went round the world
It made all the children think
There will be no toys for girls or boys
With Santa in the clink!

When George Bush heard the news
He knew just what it meant
No toys for girls, no toys for boys
No George for President!

George had written to Santa
Saying he'd been good so perhaps
He could have a kit for Christmas
To play war-games with the chaps!

He summoned all his generals
Ordered the army to stand by
Cancelled leave for all the navy
Sent the air force into the sky!

He called the G-Men to his side
Insisted they get Santa out of jail!!!
Then despatched them off to Toyland
With strict orders not to fail!

Ten squadrons circled overhead
Large tanks rolled up the street
The jailer got the message
And let Santa out tout-suite!

For now the problems over
Hopefully Santa will come by
Escorted (as far as Texas)
By fighter squadrons in the sky!

George? Congress is getting worried
(They fear some childish ruction)
If Santa should forget to leave George,
Any weapon of mass destruction!

YOU ONLY HAVE TO ASK

There must be someone I suppose,
Would like the poem I now compose,
But before I start, as you insist,
I will compile a proper list.

Then you can choose the one you like-
The vicar and his squeaking bike,
The lawyer with his legal writs,
The guy who takes your car to bits.

The auditor that checks the books,
The detective busy chasing crooks,
The painter has his paints and brushes,
The plumber with his taps and flushes.

The cowboy has his horse and saddle,
The canoeist who has just one paddle,
The new bride blushing many blushes,
The oilman with a well that gushes.

The hussy with her heart of gold,
The tramp that sleeps out in the cold,
The butcher chopping up his meat,
The copper walking on his beat.

The belly dancer, shaking, shaking,
The baker and the bread he's baking,
The grocer with his sauce and spices,
The dentist with his strange devices.

The doctor with his stethoscope,
The sailor and his mooring rope,
The seamstress with her bolts of silk,
The milkman with his bottled milk.

The gardener with his fork and spade,
The waitress serving lemonade,
The cobbler with his soles and heels,
The fisherman with jellied eels.

The soldier with his army kit,
The lady with her gin and it,
Her husband with his smoking habit,
The poacher with his dog and rabbit.

Now if you would like a poem per se-
Just say the word, - I'll start today.

*

SOMETIMES

Sometimes I can
Sometimes I can't
Sometimes I will
Sometimes I won't
Sometimes I do
Sometimes I don't
Sometimes I'm happy
Sometimes I'm sad
Sometimes I'm good
Sometimes I'm bad
Sometimes I'm certain
Sometimes I'm unsure
Sometimes I'm wrong
Sometimes I'm right
Sometimes.

THOUGHTS ON FOOD

The Scots are keen on porridge
The Irish enjoy a stew
The English order roast beef
And Yorkshire puddings too!

The Swedes adore their smorgasbord
Like the Finns and Norwegians do
The Dutch are keen on cheeses
And of course the Swiss are too!

The Italians delight in pasta
The Chinese noodles and rice
Spaniards enjoy paella
To the Portuguese sardines are nice!

The Yanks fill up on peanuts
Burgers, popcorn and hot-dogs
Sauerkrauts a German dish
But with the French it's frogs!

Canadians dine on pancakes
With bacon and fried eggs
Washed down with maple syrup
Perhaps they have hollow legs!

The Indians love their curries
Made mild or piping hot
Cannibals like many things
They cook up in a pot!

One day they cooked an admiral
And his bosun from the navy
The admiral said, "Be brave old chap"
"Aye, Aye, Sir, I have just spoiled the beggar's gravy!"

AN ODE TO THE CHEMIST

When I walk into the chemist
And happy faces see
I know that they will do their best
For whatevers ailing me.
You can be really confident
If you need pills or potions
They will have the thing you need
From aspirins to hand lotions!
Folk enquiring as well they might
When they suffer constipation
The chemist has the pills you need
(Enough to treat the nation.)
The girls are not embarrassed
When you need some advice
On how to cure your dandruff
Or an aftershave that's nice!

Should you need attention
For blisters on your toes
Perhaps you want a hankie
As you need to blow your nose.
There are many tubes of this and that
In packs both square and round
The girls know all the prices
And where they may be found!
One thing would surely please us
Let the girls all wear vests
With their names and phone numbers
Writ large upon their chests.
Next time you are in the chemist's
And you are standing in a queue
I am sure a smiling girl will ask
"What can I do for you?"

HOW ARE YOU?

"I'm fine," - what else can I say
As life grows shorter every day
Why it only seems like yesterday
I pulled our children on their sleigh
Built crumbling castles in the sand
Spent holidays in some foreign land
Went diving seeking pirate's treasure
Playing golf gave so much pleasure.

Friend filled years I now remember
Springs that lasted till September
Warm summer nights - our Bar-B-Queue
The happy chat of folks we knew
Old age has carried some away
Now silence dominates our day
Then at last the old phone rings
It's some sales girl selling things.

Then a call from morbid Clyde
To tell us another chum has died
He relates bad news with the best intention
Good news Clyde never thinks to mention
Then an invite from Will and his spouse
Eight o'clock sharp at the curry house!
On Saturday evening if you please
We are having a reunion at the new Chinese!

Somehow we find enough to do
Another week has hurried through
Sunday we are told is the day for rest
Resting is the thing that we do best
We go to church Remembrance Sundays
Christenings or some wedding fun days
Funerals of friends we always attend
And will be at our own come the very end!
Until then as life's clock ticks clack-clack
Let's enjoy ourselves- we will not be back!

THINKING BACK

When thinking back along the years
And of all the folk you have met
It must be many thousands
Yet no face will you forget.

From early kindergarten years
All through your search for knowledge
Think of all the folk you met
Till you finally left college.

The army called for six long years
Where in barracks, trains and ships
In situations you were glad
So pleased to have friendships.

The look on young men's faces
As they marched forth to do battle
Those dam uncaring politicians
Treating men like cattle.

Cheering when the war was won
Peace at last, the Armistice
So many happy dancing people
And willing girls to kiss.

They took away your toys of war
Released you back to civvy life
Back to the world of business
With so much work and strife.

Then romance comes, and marriage,
Start a family, settle down
Acquire neighbours, (and a mortgage)
And learn all about the town.

Then you join the sailing club,
Take part in the regattas
You have become a business man
It is profit now that matters.

If time passed slowly years ago
Now each day just rushes past
For me, for you, for everyone
Time keeps running, running fast.

THE SAD, SAD, SAD COYOTE BLUES

When your ever loving honey
Has run off with all your money
When you are sad and broken hearted,
Have been since your love departed.

Sing the Blues, Sing the Blues
The Sad, Sad, Sad Coyote Blues!

You feeling sorry for yourself
Because she left you on the shelf
She has really been malicious -
Left you with all those dirty dishes.

Sing the Blues, Sing the Blues
The Sad, Sad, Sad Coyote Blues!

So that calculating dolly
Has run off with all your lolly
And you are feeling oh so tense -
Nothing in your world makes sense.

Sing the blues, sing the blues –
Those Sad, Sad, Sad Coyote Blues!

Now your are minus all your gold
And your sad story has been told,
One day you will meet another
Till then join with me brother -

Sing the blues, Sing the blues –
Those Sad, Sad, Sad Coyote Blues!

THE CANDIDATE

Vote for me, Vote for Me!
Each candidate will plead
I am just the man your need!
To fight corruption, fiddles, sleaze,
Do anything you ask to please.
In the press or wherever I go
On television and the radio
Surely you have heard my boast
Of things, I think, you need the most!
In matters simple or profound
I think I am the best around!
I promise to lobby and support,
Champion, campaign, hold the fort!
Show how far my objectives range
My thoughts about cataclysmic change
I say again, corruption, fiddles, sleaze,
Everything you want but please –
Vote for me, Vote for ME!
There will be cheaper this and cheaper that,
Food to feed your dog and cat,
Cheaper wine and cheaper beer,
So many things to make you cheer.
Me, admit at feeling rueful?
When I'm not completely truthful
Five hundred promises I've made
You know I call a spade, a spade
I am the one to fight your cause-
What did you say your name was?

What will I do if not elected…?
Some other candidate is selected - ?
Off the record - between ourselves
I'll go back to stacking shelves.

WITH ALL DUE RESPECT
(A Crib Sheet for Politicians)

With all due respect -
At the end of the day -
At this moment in time -
Y'know what I mean?
When all is said and done -
You must be joking!
Like, for example,
And with all due respect -
To be absolutely honest -
I hear what you are saying.
It's not rocket science -
Just blue sky thinking -
Y'know what I mean?
So let's touch base -
Going forward together -
Between a rock and a hard place -
Taking one day at a time -
Y' know what I mean?
To be honest,
Absolutely honest,
And with all due respect -
If you get my meaning -
Just as it comes -
I hear what you are saying, but...
With the best will in the world -

In my opinion –
Y'know what I mean?
But on the other hand -
In my experience -
Take for example…
No way!
As far as it goes -
The way I remember it -
If I can come in here –
Are you sure?
It is easy to be wise after…..
You have got to be joking!
In the interest of all…..
If you get my drift..
Y'know what I mean?
If I was in your shoes…
Straight from the horse's mouth…

THE FOX

The fox
Walks up the garden
Then stops
And looks around
Ears alert and listening
For any danger sound
Refuge
Haven
Sanctuary found
Lies safe
Upon the lawn
Sleeping now
In the warming sun
Relaxed,
Content
To rest for hours
Waking
Just to groom -
Or scratch
Then back to sleep
In the midday sun
Safe
From hounds
Safe
From the hunter's gun!

For Frank on his birthday;

WELL SOMEBODY HAS TO DO IT!

Oh happy manure grader skipping on your merry way
With at least a dozen "jobs" to grade you will have a busy day.

Newly cast horse apples lie steaming on the road
And just around the corner he finds another load.

Heifers in green fields are graded "M" - for Mushy
The old bull sniffing through the bars is graded "S" for Slushy.

Should he come up behind you standing in a queue
I'll bet you fifty dollars the word you speak is "phew"!

When the grader's day is over and night begins to fall
His wife insists he leaves his muddy wellies in the hall.

At last the television ends and the Sandman softly calls
Frank slowly makes his way to bed still wearing overalls.

He dreams of cows in flush green fields
Carefully calculating their future yields.

He claims Swift Current muck is much finer
Than the stuff you get from Old Regina.

The droppings that sheep and cattle pass
Are better when they are eating grass.

When it comes to moose take care -
The same applies with grizzly bear.

Breathing fresh Sussex air I'm sure
I do not envy you the job of grading manure!

MORE BEANS FOR ANYONE?

(Progress Report)

The Chairman's message -"Our aim each week
Is to perfect more beans that are unique –

Concerning the varieties we did try -
Several reports have caught my eye.

On the bugling beans we can do no more -
They are on trial with the Armoured Corps.

The first consignment has gone down well
The tank crews report so far no smell!

The bragging bean is not quite right
It continues to sound off all day and night!

The trumpeting bean lives up to its' name
Clear sounding and savoury as we claim!

The piquant bean we know tastes good
With bacon, toast - any convenient food!

The rambling bean famous for ructation
Is available in stores across the nation!

The placid bean, calm, quiet and serene
Was enjoyed at the banquet for the Queen!

Reports the silent bean cannot be heard
That it's pungent stench is quite absurd!

The sluggard bean was languid, feckless
The fidgety bean was uneasy, restless!

The ideal bean should sound quite loud -
Yet powerful, purgatorial in any crowd!

Our business is beans - has been from the start
I believe in beans with all of my heart!

Excuse me class but I just had to blow
Control can be difficult you know.

TOMMY LOST HIS FROG TODAY

Tommy lost his frog today,
(He kept it in his pocket)
Tom was playing on the lawn
When it jumped out like a rocket!

Now Tommy did not know his frog
Had recently departed
So when he found his frog had gone
He was oh so broken hearted.

Tommy searched the garden
He looked under every stone and log
Then he asked a passing policeman,
"Please, have you seen my frog?"

"A missing frog?" said the policeman
" Now I've heard of a stray dog -
But no one has enquired before
About a missing frog."

"Give me all his details
I'll write them in my book
Because an accurate description
Will help me when I look."

"Well", said Tom "his name is Croak
I'm sure he does not bite
His eyes bulge out a little
And he stays awake all night."

"His skin is a sort of shiny green
His legs are very long
He does not care for Frenchmen
And he sings a croaking song.

The policeman and young Tommy
Searched all around the park
There was no sign of Croak the frog
And it was getting dark!

Then they heard a croaky sound
Coming from the lake
The frog chorus was warming up
Now what a noise they'll make!

There, sitting on the lily pads
They saw lots and lots of frogs.
The policeman said "Call out his name
Like people call their dogs!"

When Tommy shouted "Mr Croak!"
A hundred frogs replied
"Croak-Croak, Croak-Croak"
"Croak"- every time he tried.

Now Tommy has a new pet
He keeps it in a jar
And even if it goes astray
Well, snails don't go very far!

MY BUDDY

I recall long, long years ago
You held me close - I loved you so

Your smiling lips, your happy thoughts
The blue party dress with polka dots

Winter walks on crunching snow
Frost kissed cheeks, your eyes aglow

The warmth, the thrill of your embrace
Rubbing noses face to face

Lips shiny with warm buttered toast
You were the girl that I loved most

Lips as red as summer cherries
Ripe and full like sun-warmed berries

Your eager lips, that sudden kiss
No other love could be like this

Eyes as blue as prairie skies
Laughing eyes to idolize

Then came the war I went away
I promised to return one day

Though fate decreed another finish
My love for you will not diminish

Time will not erase the face I see
When I think of you my good buddy.

BELLA'S HOME FOR STRAY CATS

You know Auntie Bella has gone on her way
She made it to heaven despite what prudes say
She left all her millions to a home for stray cats
(Two-legged felines that prefer beds to mats!)

Aunt Bella knew of young girls who fell by the way
Of rich men who promised, then led maidens astray
Aunt Bella's great grandma, back in 1803
Was betrayed by a Colonel from the artillery!

Grandma's diaries are about cats she befriended
Of apartments lush and apartments splendid
Where kittens played games with octennial boys
Who now pay rather well for their personal joys!

Right now in Bella's Home for Stray Cats
The new vicar is naked apart from his spats
A retired major general with his membrum virile
Sweet-talks a bishop with an enticing smile!

Her daughter Mirabelle runs a very tight ship
She caters for lechers who like girls to strip
And just for the record – I really must mention
All Belles' stray cats get a very good pension!

PARKINSON'S CLOG DANCING & GLEE CLUB

"PARKINSON'S PARODY"
Sung to Cornish Folk Melody

The consultant said to me today
Your Parkinson's is here and here to stay
So I think it's right that you should know -
Whatever we do it will not go!
It will not go!

(Neuro Nurse's Chorus:)

Do not worry, - do not fret
We are in control with Sinemet!

There are scores of maladies we can cure
Plus numerous ailments of this we're sure
The wisest thing when you feel ill
Is catch something cured by a simple pill!
By a simple pill!

Do not worry, - do not pine
We are in control with Selegiline!

Parkinson's is faithful my good friend
And will stay with you until the very end
Enjoy your life and be as happy as you can
Ignore the fellow with his little black van!
Little black van!

Do not worry, - do not fret
We are in control with Sinemet!

Do not worry, - do not pine
We also prescribing Selegiline!

(Consultants, Doctors, Neuro Nurse's Chorus,
Branch Committee's Harmony Concordia)

If you get worried – do not despair,
Just call us and we'll all be there!

We'll be there-
You know we care-

*

RONNIE

My buddy's name is Ronnie
I know him very well
He is a touch too bad for heaven
And he is far too good for hell
He is somewhere in the middle
Trying as hard as any man
Hoping he will be a winner
And not just an also-ran
But when his chips are counted
The golden gates will open wide
A voice will say, "You gave your best
So Ronald, come inside"

THE SOUTHDOWN KID

The Southdown Kid rode into town
With only one intention
To satisfy his lustful ways
With girls we will not mention.

As news of his arrival got around
The girls, who were not prude
Left their shops and offices
And very quickly queued.

A score of happy maidens
And then a sign of trouble
The thing of which the Kid was proud
Right now was bending double.

It crossed his mind his loving Mum -
He could not be mistaken
Had sprinkled lots of bromide
On his sausage, eggs and bacon.

One darling, ever eager girl
W ho lived down at the Cloisters
Hurried to the fish shop
And bought six dozen oysters.

I am pleased to say she saved the day
The Kid's no longer bent
Four score maidens went their way
All happy and content.

He wed that darling eager girl
They are as happy as can be -
She sprinkles bromide on his toast,
His lunch and in his tea.

But when the moment takes her
She hurries to the Cloisters
She knows what's going to happen
When he has enjoyed his meal of oysters!

*

THE VICAR

When the vicar comes to tea
He eats ten times as much as me
Ten times the sandwiches, ten times the ham,
Ten times the jelly and ten times the jam
Ten times the cookies, ten times the cake,
I just hope he gets ten times my tummy ache.

"LITHPERING FRANK SMITH" – THE REAL STORY.

To a snow bank on the prairie
From all the united nations
They came admiring and applauding
Frank's wonderful creations,
They read the words in wonder
Letters bold and so refined
Now another wonder for the world
Was forming in his mind!

The words he spoke you know so well
"Friends, Canucks, Countrymen!
Lend me your ears
I come to write a message
It should take some twenty beers –
So stand aside and let me start
I've learned the words all off by heart
I will not need your pencil
Even though it be a Venus
I'd rather stick to my old friend –
I'll use my faithful penis!"

Then he strode to the virgin snowbank
All new and shining white
Then he started pithing
Oh how that man could write!
He carried on all afternoon
And kept on through the night
Then on that bright December morn
When all was crisp and cold.

They saw writ in letters large
Each standing clear and gold-

"PITHING LESSONS TWENTY DOLLARS
HALF PRICE FOR VETERANS AND FOR SCHOLARS"

Signed – "Frank Smith pitheth thith"

*

WHAT HAPPENED?

What happened to the girl I wed
Sleeping now in her lover's bed
The wife I spent those years adoring -
I expect he puts up with her snoring!

*

PLEASE MY LOVE

Please my love be very gentle
Because I feel so sentimental
Dreaming sweet dreams of you -
The wonderful things we used to do
Many years have gone by - alas
We keep our false teeth in a glass!